A DEFINING MOMENT IN HISTORY

*Prophetic Words for the
United States of America*

NATHAN SHAW

"I still believe in America.
I still believe in the land of liberty.
God's got a plan for America.
I only pray America will see."

Steve Grace
Australian Singer/Songwriter
From *Song for America*

CONTENTS

PROLOGUE:
A DEFINING MOMENT

Many years ago God put the United States of America on my heart. Since 2016 I have felt compelled to write, prophesy, declare and decree concerning the nation. This book brings together my prophetic writings for the United States. I am from New Zealand. I am not from the United States. I love New Zealand, but it has been at times frustrating that I am not also a citizen of the United States. I want to be there and shout what God has shown me from the rooftops. I want to have my feet on the ground so that I can do whatever I can to help shift and change history.

I am reminded of a poor widow who seemed helpless to initiate change in Israel. Jesus commended her for giving two small coins into the temple treasury. The two coins were all she had. All I have is two little fire sticks: pen and paper. Used in the right way, fire-sticks can ignite raging fires. It is my earnest prayer that these simple words can be used to in some way ignite prophetic destiny within the United States and call forth a radical generation of freedom fighters.

Other than minor grammatical changes, and slight improvements for clarity or flow, each chapter appears as it was originally released. Some chapters speak to nations in a general way but were particularly directed to the United States. Each chapter can be read alone or the flow of revelation can be followed from beginning to end.

2020 has been marked by a corona-virus pandemic, nationwide shut-downs, unprecedented economic challenges, issues of race relations, rioting and an increasingly intense political landscape. As I write it is only a few days since the death of Supreme Court Justice, Ruth Bader Ginsburg on September the 18th, 2020. That date is significant on two counts: Firstly it is Rosh Hashanah, the Jewish New Year. Secondly it is just 46 days before the presidential election on November 3rd, 2020. Psalm 46 is truly a prophetic Psalm for this season. Ruth Bader Ginsburg's passing has ratcheted the intense unrest within the United States to an even greater level and it is unlikely to abate. With all these issues simultaneously in the public consciousness the issue of justice is fairly and squarely on the table.

It doesn't take a prophet to discern the obvious: This is a defining moment. Many things hang in the balance. I am concerned that too many prophets are prophesying judgment and not properly understanding legacy. There is a phenomenal legacy in the United States and God watches over it jealously. Even when we are unfaithful, He remains faithful. I am convinced that the best is yet to come.

The United States' greatest days of glory are still ahead, but that doesn't mean there won't be a battle. That's where you come in. The greater the battle, the more glorious the victory. It truly is time for unprecedented vision. Let's go!

THE FOUNDATION OF FREEDOM

(Released 7th August 2014)

Freedom is in the foundation of the United States. Freedom was in the hearts of her founders. Freedom was promoted, established and protected through her Constitution. Freedom overflowed her towns and cities during the First and Second Great Awakenings. Because of this the United States has been blessed like few nations in history. And this freedom hasn't only stayed within her shores. From the United States great freedom has gone forth that has blessed the nations. But also from the United States much evil has gone forth that has ensnared the nations. With the privilege of great freedom came great responsibility. Freedom spent wrongly led to selfishness, carnality and perversion.

Prophetic voices have sounded repeatedly to warn the United States to turn from her present course. If she doesn't she will lose much of her freedom and much of her authority in the nations. The United States is young. Unquestionably she has had significant impact but she has by no means fulfilled her ultimate destiny. The nation will experience significant shakings. Prophets of doom will arise and discourage many. But God *has* not and *will* not give up on the United States.

God loves this nation because He loves freedom and He loves people. The United States embraced and welcomed the nations. It has residents from nations all over the world. Throughout its short history a cry for freedom has always come before God's throne from her shores. God will respond to the cry of these faithful intercessors. They have stood in the gap in pulpits, in wars, in governments, in schools, in homes, in Hollywood, on the streets, from public platforms and in hiddenness. Their prayers, their actions, their labors of love and their sacrifices have not gone unnoticed.

Out of the shakings will come a renewed spirit and a fierce resolve. Freedom fighters will take a stand for a freedom that does not compromise responsibility. A new breed of spiritual and political leader will arise. These brave voices will seem small and insignificant to many but God's favor will be on them. Ultimately their voices will prevail. Rather than rail at the sins of the nation they will tell her who she is. Rather than despair at the nation's loss of direction they will prophesy her ultimate destiny. Pray for these freedom fighters! Through them the nation will come to value the responsibility of freedom and walk in her God ordained destiny. In the midst of the shakings do not despair. The best is yet to come.

IT'S GONNA BE HUGE!

Recently I saw an interview with Republican presidential nominee, Donald Trump. I particularly noticed Trump's phrase, *"It's gonna be HUGE!"* A few weeks later I was praying for this generation and I heard God say, *"It's gonna be HUGE!"* Suddenly the phrase was loaded with prophetic significance. Huge shifts are about to take place in the nations—both politically and spiritually. God has a plan for the nations and he is strategically positioning them like chess pieces on a chess board. God gave me two words that describe many of the shifts that are about to happen. The two words were "unexpected" and "unconventional."

God starts revolutions in ways we don't expect and he often uses the most unlikely characters to do it. Two thousand years ago a solitary figure came on the scene and initiated a revolution that radically changed the world. John the Baptist's ministry was unexpected and unconventional. The impact was phenomenal. There was no good reason why John the Baptist should have gained the attention of the nation of Israel. His ministry was based in the remote regions around the Jordan river. He wasn't polished. His clothing was primitive. His lifestyle was unconventional. Despite the things stacked against him, all of Judea and Jerusalem came to hear him. And more than that—

they were so moved by his message that they responded with dramatic life style changes (Mark 1:5-6).

The religious leaders of the day struggled to define John the Baptist. He didn't fit the boxes they were expecting. They found the situation so perplexing that they sent people to inquire of John personally.

Now this is the testimony of John, when the Jews sent priests and Levites from Jerusalem to ask him, "Who are you?" He confessed, and did not deny, but confessed, "I am not the Christ." And they asked him, "What then? Are you Elijah?" He said, "I am not." "Are you the Prophet?" And he answered, "No." Then they said to him, "Who are you, that we may give an answer to those who sent us? What do you say about yourself?" He said: "I am the voice of one crying in the wilderness" (John 1:19-23).

John was not confused about his identity. He knew who he was. He was a prophetic voice *crying* in the wilderness. John didn't come with a theology—he came with a cry. His cry was so impacting it shook individuals, institutions, civil authorities and religious systems. John didn't come with the authority of a well reasoned argument—he came with the authority of deep humility.

What does it mean to be a voice *crying* in the wilderness? Consider:

- A cry is not just a sound—it has substance. It comes with the force of divine revelation— revelation imprinted so deeply on the messenger's heart that it becomes part of who they are.

- A cry carries the sound of eternity. It comes from another realm.
- A cry has a frequency that changes the atmosphere. It causes the rival kingdoms of light and darkness to clash.
- A cry bypasses the mind and penetrates the human spirit. John's voice penetrated defenses and excuses and demanded a response (Luke 3:7).

John's cry riveted people's attention on Jesus—the Lamb of God (John 1:29,36).

John's public ministry only lasted a short time. It was quickly overshadowed by the ministry of Jesus Himself. However Jesus' Apostles understood the huge significance of John's ministry. Consider the following scenario:

- Judas betrayed Jesus and then hung himself.
- Within a short time Peter announced that another person must be selected to take the place of Judas.
- Peter made it clear that the person selected needed to be a witness of the whole time period from John's baptism until Jesus' ascension— **"Therefore, of these men who have accompanied us all the time that the Lord Jesus went in and out among us, *beginning from the baptism of John* to that day when He was taken up from us, one of these must become a witness with us of His resurrection" (Acts 1:21-22 Italics added).**

Notice that Peter says, "*Beginning* from the baptism of John." John the Baptist's cry was the beginning of a revolution that radically and permanently shook and changed nation after nation. In fact, the revolution continues today.

Few people appreciate the impact of John's ministry during his lifetime—a whole nation was stirred and awakened, religious leaders were perplexed and confused, even the irreligious king Herod was fascinated by John's preaching. The Wuest translation of Mark 6:20 brings out the subtlety of the original Greek—**"and, having heard** [John the Baptist] **often, [Herod] was in a continual state of perplexity, and he was in the habit of hearing him with pleasure."** The heart of this ruthless and ungodly king was divided. He was attracted to the cry but repelled by the conviction. Even the ungodly were stirred by the sound of eternity in John's cry.

Fast forward twenty years. A teacher called Apollos visited the city of Ephesus in Asia Minor:

Now a certain Jew named Apollos, born at Alexandria, an eloquent man and mighty in the Scriptures, came to Ephesus. This man had been instructed in the way of the Lord; and being fervent in spirit, he spoke and taught accurately the things of the Lord, though he knew only the baptism of John. So he began to speak boldly in the synagogue (Acts 18:24-26).

Apollos knew only the baptism of John and yet twenty years after John's ministry he was "fervent in spirit" and "spoke boldly." Not long after this the Apostle Paul visited the city of Ephesus. There he found disciples that had never heard of the Holy Spirit. They only knew the baptism of John (Acts 19:1-7). John the Baptist's cry was having an impact in far away nations even twenty years after his death!

Fast forward to the modern day. American society was significantly shaped by the First and Second Great Awakenings of the 18th and 19th centuries. The First Great Awakening was sparked by the ministry of English preacher, George Whitefield. George Whitefield came with a cry that awakened people from lifeless, ritualistic religion. His emphasis was a living, dynamic, and intensely personal relationship with God. Awakenings are a lot bigger than revivals. Revivals are glorious. Awakenings are HUGE. They change the destiny of nations by permanently changing the mindsets, perspectives and attitudes of the majority. Revivals tend to impact the Church or particular regions. Awakenings shift and shape whole nations.

Two recent ministries that had a powerful impact on my life personally were Leonard Ravenhill and Jill Austin. Leonard Ravenhill and Jill Austin weren't polished theologians but they both had a radical cry for revival and fresh encounters with God. It was this cry that stirred and awakened my heart to experience and know God in a real way. It is this same cry that will awaken the present generation. John the Baptist is a prophetic model foreshadowing multitudes of world changers that God is raising up in our generation. Multiply the prophetic cries of John the Baptist, George Whitefield, Leonard Ravenhill, Jill Austin and a multitude of others and you will begin to get the picture.

The good news of God's kingdom disturbs and disrupts earthly structures and earthly thinking. It starts with a prophetic cry that challenges the status quo. For thirty years John the Baptist was unknown to the multitudes. During this time God was preparing him in hiddenness. Many are being prepared by God right now. When they come on the scene it will be unexpected. We must be prepared for the unexpected and the unconventional. These messengers will arise not only in the Church but also in every sphere of society. Structures will shake. Lives will be transformed. The kingdom will advance.

It's gonna be HUGE!

PRAYING FOR THE U.S. ELECTION AND BEYOND

(Released 26ᵗʰ October 2016)

During the third presidential debate between Donald Trump and Hillary Clinton, God prompted me to pray. Many years ago God placed the United States on my heart. On a personal level I have been blessed by many ministries that have come from the United States. On an international level I believe there is a high calling on the United States to release a Kingdom standard into the nations of the earth. This call is fiercely contended.

As I started to pray, God gave me a picture of Aaron and Hur holding up the arms of Moses. The image is from Exodus chapter 17. Israel was engaged in a fierce battle with the Amalekites. Moses went up on a hill with Aaron and Hur and raised his shepherd's rod over the battlefield. As long as Moses kept his rod raised, the battle turned in favor of the Israelites. When he lowered his rod, the battle went in favor of the Amalekites. Eventually Moses' natural strength waned and he was no longer able to hold up his rod. Aaron and Hur came to the rescue. Moses sat on a large stone, while Aaron and Hur held up his arms. The result: The Israelites soundly defeated the Amalekites.

The key to victory was Moses' rod. The rod was an indispensable tool-of-the-trade for every shepherd. A rod by itself doesn't have the authority to win a battle. Although the rod belonged to Moses, the authority came from God. The battle between Israel and the Amalekites was both a physical and a spiritual battle.

- Joshua had to lead natural soldiers against the enemy.
- Moses had to extend spiritual authority over the battlefield.

In this U.S. election there is both a ground warfare and a spiritual warfare. Both are strategically important. Voting and campaigning are ground warfare. Prayer and proclamation are spiritual warfare.

What has Moses' rod to do with the U.S. election, you might ask? Consider the following. Lance Wallnau received an invitation to go to Trump Tower with a group of leading evangelicals (see *God's Chaos Candidate* by Lance Wallnau). At the meeting Lance started to sense an anointing from God on Donald Trump. After the meeting God said to Lance, *"Read Isaiah 45."* Isaiah 45 starts out, **"Thus saith the Lord to Cyrus, My anointed..."** Cyrus was a foreign king who was instrumental in the release of Israel from captivity. He was also instrumental in releasing resources, protection, and favor so that Israel could rebuild their temple. God anointed a foreign king to do His work!

God gave me two words that describe many of the leaders He is raising up. The words were "unexpected" and "unconventional." These two words also describe Cyrus rather well. Cyrus' rise to authority was unexpected. His leadership style was unconventional. Usually leaders of large empires destroyed and subjugated other nations, Cyrus was different. The Greek historian Herodotus tells the story of how Cyrus came to power. It is a fascinating and unique against-the-odds story. God shaped Cyrus' heart through some very unique circumstances. After Cyrus was in power God gave him Daniel—a trained and godly statesman—to help him administrate the empire.

God gave Moses authority. God gave Cyrus authority. If Lance Wallnau is correct, God has given Donald Trump a unique authority to bring restoration and freedom in the United States. But Moses wasn't able to bring victory against the Amalekites single-handedly. When Moses' weakness prevented him from raising his rod, Aaron and Hur had to support him. Because the battle was drawn out, Moses' weakness became obvious. Moses needed help to hold up his rod of authority. One of the primary purposes of intercession is to support those God has endowed with authority. If we recognize that God has given Trump a unique authority for the United States, it is our responsibility to uphold and support him through intercession.

Before Moses led Israel out of captivity, he spent forty years living in the Sinai wilderness. It took unique skill to live in that environment. His rod was a testimony to his natural experience and skill. The nation of Israel needed this unique experience and skill in their leader because of the unique territory they had to traverse. Likewise, Donald Trump has a staff. His staff is his unique experience and skill. This experience and skill are important for the United States because of the unique territory she will traverse in the coming years.

As I continued to pray for the presidential debate, God led me to take authority over the airwaves. I felt a very strong authority to do this. There is a battle over the airwaves. This battle is to do with how things are heard and perceived. Words travel through airwaves. Audio and video are transmitted through airwaves. Whoever dominates the airwaves in a nation wins the battle for the minds of those in that nation. Interestingly, in Ephesians 2:2, Satan is called the ruler of the authority of the air.

We can take authority over the airwaves by blessing that which the enemy is cursing and honoring that which the enemy is dishonoring. The tabernacle of David was known for continual praise and proclamation. This praise and proclamation dominated the airwaves (the spirit realm) over the nation of Israel. This in turn shifted the mindset of the nation. When the enemy dominates the airwaves in a nation, ungodly agendas are heard and magnified. When righteousness dominates the airwaves in a nation, righteous agendas are heard and magnified.

As I continued to pray, I found myself calling forth a new sound. Once again there was great authority to do this. When a new sound comes forth the dialogue changes. The election campaign has become very focused on personal attacks about Trump's or Clinton's ability to lead. The enemy is using this focus to hide his bigger agenda. I was encouraged to find out that the very real issue of abortion came up at the end of the debate. This election is not primarily about Trump versus Clinton. It is about something much more serious. There are two forces contending for the United States. The real conflict is the culture of life versus the culture of death. The culture of death has already taken much ground in the nation.

Finally, as I was praying, I saw an angel blowing a trumpet of change. I responded by calling forth change over the nation.

On November the 8th, 2016 the United States has a decision to make. I pray that she makes the right decision. The U.S. election is not, however, the end of the conflict between the culture of life and the culture of death. The outcome of this election is hugely significant for this battle. But no matter the outcome, we must continue to fight for the culture of death to be stopped, and the culture of life to be established.

Through prayer, intercession, praise and proclamation let us recognize and uphold those God has anointed. Let us boldly take authority over the airwaves. Let us confidently call forth a new sound. Let us intentionally call forth the culture of life. And let us resolutely declare and call forth change over the nation.

ANZUS, THE EAST GATE, AND THE ALIGNMENT OF THE NATIONS

(Released 20th January 2017)

God has a plan to bless the nations. The enemy has a plan to pre-empt chaos in the nations. It is not time for end-time chaos. One of the main ways the enemy brings chaos is by turning nations against Israel. God promised Abraham that his descendants would become a great nation. That promise was fulfilled in the nation of Israel. God made an additional promise to Abraham: The nations who blessed Israel would be blessed, but the nations who cursed Israel would be cursed (Genesis 12:1-3). The enemies plan is to turn nations against Israel. God's plan is to turn nations toward Israel. God is working to bring the nations into alignment with His purposes.

THE EAST GATE

Three years ago I woke up at 4:44 in the morning and then went straight back to sleep. The second time it happened I realized that God was speaking to me. In Ezekiel 44:4, Ezekiel sees the glory of God enter the temple through the east gate. God began to give me an understanding of the significance of the east gate. There are many "east gate" cities in the earth. They are significant because they are entry points for God's glory to flood the nations. God showed me that New Zealand would become an "east gate" nation.

New Zealand is the furthest nation from Israel. Isaiah prophesied: **"Sing to the LORD a new song, and His praise *from the ends of the earth*, you who go down to the sea, and all that is in it, you coastlands and you inhabitants of them!" (Isaiah 42:10 italics added).** Isaiah and Habakkuk both prophesied that the earth would be filled with the knowledge of the glory of the LORD as the waters cover the sea (Isaiah 11:9, Habakkuk 2:14). I believe that when the "east gate" of New Zealand and the "east gate" of Jerusalem are both open an arc of glory will cover the globe.

In September 2016 I was invited to speak at a conference in Brisbane, Australia. As I sought the Lord for this conference He showed me that Brisbane was an "east gate" city and that the spiritual connection between New Zealand and Australia would be a powerful "east gate" that would link with Jerusalem. I shared this at the conference. A seer friend of mine was sitting toward the back of the meeting. She was recording the meeting on her cell phone. Not far from her a young boy kept interceding and crying out, *"Open the gate! Open the gate!"* His cry was clearly captured on the cell phone recording. Although I was talking about the "east gate" of New Zealand and Australia, I didn't use the specific phrase, "Open the gate." The young boy received that intercessory cry straight from the Spirit.

ANZUS

Two months later God spoke to me and said, *"ANZUS will live again."* ANZUS is an acronym of the words Australia, New Zealand, United States. ANZUS was originally a three way defense pact made between these nations. It was formed in 1951. In 1986 the ANZUS agreement was hindered between New Zealand and the United States when New Zealand initiated a nuclear-free zone in its territorial waters. The treaty still exists between Australia and New Zealand and between Australia and the United States. (Interestingly, the Royal New Zealand Navy invited the United States Navy to send a vessel to participate in their 75th birthday celebrations held in November 2016. The USS *Sampson* became the first US warship to visit New Zealand in 33 years. However, because of the large Kaikoura earthquake in central New Zealand the USS *Sampson* proceeded directly to Kaikoura to provide humanitarian assistance. I believe this event is prophetic and that the United States will come to New Zealand's aid in a future time of great need).

After God spoke to me I asked Him for greater clarity and understanding—*"God what do you mean when You say, 'ANZUS will live again?'"* I don't know the exact details, timing, or form of this alliance, but I believe it includes standing with Israel. Australia and New Zealand played a significant and united role in the capturing of Beersheba and Jerusalem in 1917, and the United States has strongly supported Israel since it became a nation in 1948.

STADIUM DREAM

Early in January 2017 I had a dream. In the dream I was in the middle of a large sports field. The field was surrounded by a massive multi-tiered stadium. The grandstands were covered but the field was not. I was alone and sitting on a make shift portable film directors seat. I was reminded of Peter Jackson, the director of *The Lord of the Rings* and *The Hobbit* movies. These movies were filmed in New Zealand and feature New Zealand's stunning scenery. I knew that there was a very significant event on at the stadium that night. Next thing a helicopter flew down into the field. In the helicopter was a married couple I know from New Zealand who have a prophetic ministry to the nations and do intercessory tours to Israel. They had come to do a television interview with me about the event that was happening that night. I was self conscious about being interviewed because my hair was out of place. I wasn't prepared for or expecting a television interview.

As the dream ended I saw the numbers "33:3" and then the word "Isaiah" came in front of the numbers. I remember thinking in the dream, *"That's odd, normally 33:3 would be Jeremiah, not Isaiah."* In Jeremiah 33:3 God says, **"Call to Me, and I will answer you, and show you great and mighty things, which you do not know."** When I woke from the dream I looked up Isaiah 33:3. It is about God defending and protecting Israel from hostile nations: **"At the noise of the tumult the people shall flee; When You lift Yourself up, the nations shall be scattered."** Jeremiah 33:3 is about intercession and prophetic vision. Isaiah 33:3 is about Israel. In this dream I believe I represented intercessory ministry.

TELL-A-VISION

Many people believe that political forces, empowered by demonic agendas, are dictating the ultimate direction of the nations. This is not true. Intercessory ministry has more authority than political forces and demonic agendas (Revelation 8:3-5). I am reminded of Derek Prince's classic book, *Changing History Through Prayer and Fasting*. We should not be intimidated by political and demonic forces. Most intercessory ministry is done in secret. Intercessors are not looking for the limelight and would rather not be interviewed for television, however, their voice will be heard and released through the airwaves. Prophetically television can mean tell-a-vision. Intercessors will declare *God's* vision for the nations. What was the big event in my dream? I believe the cloud of witnesses spoken of in Hebrews 12:1 are watching the events in the nations. They are particularly interested in the "east gate" of New Zealand/Australia.

I believe there will be an ANZUS alliance that will stand with Israel. At the moment Australia stands in strong support of Israel. Donald Trump, the newly elected president of the United States, also stands in strong support of Israel. What of New Zealand? In December 2016 New Zealand co-sponsored a United Nations resolution that effectively made it illegal for Israel to build on occupied territory or for Jews to live in the Jewish quarter of Jerusalem. As soon as the resolution passed Israel withdrew it's ambassador to New Zealand. I believe it is God's purpose for Australia, New Zealand and the United States to form a three corded strand of support for Israel. The "33:3" in my dream also speaks of these three nations. Consider the following:

- Three nations. The alignment of Australia, New Zealand and the United States with Israel will help bring many other nations into alignment with Israel. God is prompting intercessors from around the world to pray for New Zealand (and of course other nations) to come into alignment with His agenda for Israel.
- Three is the number of resurrection. Jesus rose on the third day. When the dividing wall between Jew and Gentile comes down it will be "life from the dead" (Romans 11:15).
- The apostolic mandate given by Jesus to His disciples had three levels to it: (1) Jerusalem. (2) Judea and Samaria. (3) The ends of the earth (Acts 1:8). This order will reverse and go from the ends of the earth, back to Jerusalem. The apostolic gospel will have a powerful impact on both Jews and Palestinians.

God's plan is to align the nations with Israel. His desire is to *bless* the nations. It is time for the church to step into her intercessory prophetic role and boldly call forth God's purposes for the nations. All of heaven is watching. It's gonna be HUGE!!!

GOD'S PLANS FOR THE NATIONS – DAPHNE TAYLOR

(Dream given in April 2017)

In my dream I found myself above the world. I was with God and looking down over the world. I did not see God but I knew I was beside Him. He showed me the larger land masses and I could see separate areas with boundary lines dividing up continents and states within the land. I was too high to determine exactly which countries each land mass was. The land was lifted up out of the sea. Next I saw large groups of people, not individuals, but outlines of crowds. They were all moving different ways over many boundary lines. Some were moving with negative intent, some were simply caught up in the moving crowds, a small portion moved with purpose. I was disturbed to see such confusion and evil intent among so many people.

I asked God, *"Where are the Christians and what are they doing about this situation?"* It all looked one sided to me. I felt God smile at me with such indescribable love. Instantly my terrified thoughts changed. I had the courage to look again and I saw God's right hand covering different areas. God turned His hand onto its side and then I could see small groups of people in tightly knit groups everywhere among the nations.

God separately exposed these groups one by one until a peace returned to me. I asked God, *"Why are there not as many Christians as the other large groups that are moving about?"* He replied, *"I know these people."*

As I watched I tried to work out what the outcome of all this movement might be so I asked God, *"What is the President doing about all of this?"* I saw some illegal activity going on in the big groups. *"Does Mr. Trump even know what's going on in his own country?"* I felt God say, *"Mr. Trump knows and sees all this but he doesn't have my mandate—yet."* God was not anxious like I was.

*****

Daphne's dream went on to reveal God's glorious plans for Australia and New Zealand.

I believe that President Trump will find himself in a position like Samson in Judges 15 where his hands are tied and it looks like imminent defeat (Judges 15:9-15). God's Spirit will empower and inspire him to use a strategy that is both unexpected and unusual. It will totally turn the situation around and cause people to acknowledge God's mandate on him.

Daphne comes from Christchurch, New Zealand, where she attends Living Waters Christian Centre. She is married to Bryce. They have three children and fifteen grandchildren.

A NEW SOUND AND A NEW SEASON

(Released 25th August 2017)

The political situation in the United States is full of contention and strife. The primary issue is not politics. There is a spiritual battle raging. The real issue is the destiny of a nation. Into this situation God is calling His people to exercise priestly authority. Priests have spiritual authority (1 Peter 2:5, 9, Revelation 1:6, 5:10). In praying for the United States God led me to do two things:

- Call forth a new sound.
- Take authority over the air waves.

CALLING FORTH A NEW SOUND

The Bible talks about a new song (Psalm 33:3, 40:3, 96:1, 98:1, 144:9, 149:1, Isaiah 42:10, Revelation 5:9, 14:3). Interestingly this new song is connected with a change in the atmosphere and a change in spiritual government. Israel's King David carried this new song. He was used by God to call forth a new sound over the nation of Israel. Contention and strife were replaced by proclamation and praise. The atmosphere over

Israel changed dramatically. The destructive force of internal conflict that was tearing the nation apart was replaced by a national resolve to confront their true enemies.

As I began to call forth a new sound over the United States a powerful spiritual authority came on me. I started doing something I had never done before. It was like I was reaching into President Trump's voice and pulling out the new sound. With authority I kept reaching in and declaring, *"I call forth the new sound! I call forth the new sound!"* As we pray like this the new sound will come forth with greater authority, anointing and clarity. We have authority to call forth a new sound over the President, the Congress, the Senate, the Supreme Court, the Media, and the Church.

TAKING AUTHORITY OVER THE AIR WAVES

The second thing God led me to do was to take authority over the air waves. Spiritual government is released through air waves. Air waves carry voices, sounds and attitudes. These voices, sounds and attitudes become seeds that bring forth a harvest. Satan is called the prince of the authority (Greek "exousia") of the air (Ephesians 2:2). But Satan is not the only authority operating. There is also the authority of the new sound which carries both the government and the heart of God.

In the book of Ephesians Paul highlights the real battle—**For we do not wrestle against flesh and blood, but against principalities, against powers, against the rulers of the darkness of this age, against spiritual hosts of wickedness in the heavenly places (Ephesians 6:12).** The battlefield where this "wrestling" takes place is the air waves. That's why the weapon that combats demonic agendas is the sword of the Spirit—the word of God wielded with authority and anointing (Ephesians 6:17). God's word carries His government and His heart.

When demonic agendas are clamoring for attention they dominate the air waves and leave little room for anything else. We can take authority over the air waves so that they are cleared and set apart for godly agendas. We don't have to be intimidated by the contentious sounds that are coming from the media, the government, or the arts. The priestly authority God gives us is much greater.

A NEW SEASON

When Israel stepped into the land of Canaan they entered into a new season. With this new season there was a different sound. While they wandered in the wilderness for forty years things were relatively calm. They lived under a continual grace from God that released the basic provisions that they needed. They spent this time in barren and sparsely occupied regions. This meant that they caused little contention with other nations. When Israel stepped into Canaan this changed. Now there was an anointing to possess the land. Israel moved from maintenance anointing to change agent anointing. That was a big shift. It caused an uproar. Change often does.

The United States is in a season of change. For some it can seem like God was in the relative calm and quiet of the previous season and not in the uproar and chaos of the new season. But realize that sometimes chaos is actually caused by God. It's time to move into the new season. Don't be intimidated by the chaos. Step into your priestly authority and call forth God's purposes. Call forth the new sound. Take authority over the air waves. Foundations are shaking and will continue to shake. Old foundations will unravel and disintegrate. New foundations will come forth. God is setting things up for a great awakening. Great shaking will be followed by great awakening. It's gonna be HUGE!

A NEW GENERATION OF FREEDOM FIGHTERS

(Released 10th May 2019)

Christians are called to be peacemakers (Matthew 5:9). A peacemaker is often required to confront various people and situations. One of the biggest confrontations in the Bible was between Elijah and King Ahab. Elijah confronted Ahab directly. He boldly declared that there would be no rain except at his word. No rain meant no harvest. No harvest meant no provision. The confrontation was over Israel's source of provision. There were two options: Baal, the god of the storm cloud; or Yahweh, the God who rides the clouds (Deuteronomy 33:26, Psalm 68:4). Israel had fallen to the worship of Baal and looked to him as their source of provision.

TWO SEATS OF GOVERNMENT: HEAVENLY AND EARTHLY

When Elijah confronted Ahab there was a clash between two seats of government. Elijah stood before God and His heavenly court. Ahab presided over an earthly court. Elijah came from the heavenly court and addressed the earthly court: **And Elijah**

the Tishbite, of the inhabitants of Gilead, said to Ahab, "As the LORD God of Israel lives, before whom I stand, there shall not be dew nor rain these years, except at my word" (1 Kings 17:1).

A seat of government is concerned with the provision and protection of its subjects. Rain meant harvest and provision. No rain meant no harvest and no provision. That's why Ahab referred to Elijah as the troubler of Israel. Ahab was in fact the true troubler of Israel. He was the one who allowed Queen Jezebel to promote the worship of Baal (1 Kings 18:17-18).

There were two groups of prophets in Israel at the time. The false prophets numbered 850. The true prophets numbered only 100. 400 of the false prophets ate at Jezebel's table. In contrast, the true prophets were hidden in caves with only basic rations (1 Kings 18:4, 19).

TWO MOUNTAINS: CARMEL AND HOREB

After three years of no rain, Elijah confronted not only Ahab, but also the false prophets and the entire nation. The place of the confrontation was Mount Carmel. The challenge: to call down fire on a sacrificial animal. The false prophets were given plenty of time to beseech Baal. Regardless, there was no fire— not even a spark. Elijah called on the Lord and fire instantly consumed his sacrifice. The prophets of Baal were seized and killed. Rain clouds started to gather. Elijah went to confront Jezebel herself but was overcome with fear and fled for his life (1 Kings 18:1-19:3).

Elijah believed he was the only true prophet of God in Israel (1 Kings 18:22, 19:10, 14). He seemed unaware of the 100 prophets hidden in caves and the 7000 Israelites who did not worship Baal (1 Kings 19:18). If Jezebel couldn't destroy the true prophets the spiritual force that she wielded worked to isolate them from each other. If Elijah knew that he wasn't alone, would he have successfully defeated Jezebel? Defeating Jezebel would have been a great victory, but another question needs to be asked. If Jezebel was defeated, were the righteous ready to fill the vacuum? When there is a vacuum in spiritual government it needs to be filled. If the righteous were not ready another Jezebel could have risen, possibly even worse than the first one.

Elijah fled to Mount Horeb where he met with God. God commissioned him to anoint Hazael as king of Syria, Jehu as king of Israel, and Elisha as a prophet in his place (1 Kings 19:3-17). The right freedom fighters needed to be in place to bring about a complete victory over Jezebel. The commissioning of freedom fighters was as important as the direct confrontation that happened at Mount Carmel. Carmel was about confrontation. Horeb was about commissioning.

After the defeat of the prophets of Baal at Carmel there was a significant change in the spiritual atmosphere over the nation. True prophets were able to come out of hiding (see 1 Kings 20:35, 41, 2 Kings 2:3, 5, 7, 15, 4:38, 6:1). At the time Elijah didn't understand the significance of the victory. He was too overcome with fear and fleeing for his life. Victories can often look like defeats and defeats can often look like victories. Elijah's confrontation of the false prophets at Carmel led to his encountering God at Horeb. The mandate Elijah received at Horeb led to the commissioning of a new generation of freedom fighters.

UNDERSTANDING THE TIMES

Huge confrontations are happening in the nations of the earth. It is a strategic time. Many things that appear one way will turn out to be completely the opposite. Only those who correctly discern the clash between God's heavenly court and the respective earthly courts will interpret events correctly. Confrontations are necessary but don't miss the commissioning that is also happening. In the midst of chaos, confusion, and partial victories, God is anointing and commissioning a new generation of freedom fighters.

REMOVING JEZEBEL'S INFLUENCE FROM THE LAND

(Released 12th July 2019)

The word "Jezebel" has been used as a catch-all word to describe controlling forces and people. "Jezebel's" objective is to hinder and destroy God's purposes over individuals, churches, ministries and nations. King Ahab and his Phoencian wife, Queen Jezebel, ruled the northern kingdom of Israel during the 9th century B.C. Ahab and Jezebel were ruthless. They would do whatever was necessary to get what they wanted, even if it meant destroying the inheritance of others (1 Kings 21:1-16). Ahab was the seventh Israelite king who "did evil in the eyes of the Lord," however, under Ahab and Jezebel the level of rebellion increased dramatically. Rebellion against God became entrenched in every arena of Israel's national life. Removing Jezebel's influence from the land involved much more than simply removing Jezebel.

It's easy to see the influence of Jezebelic forces today. They work systematically to distance nations from God. One of the major battles of our times is over the destiny of the United States of America. The reason is obvious: The outcome of this battle will set the world stage for decades to come. The battle is fierce and few understand what is necessary to remove

"Jezebel's" influence from the land. This is not just an issue of casting out a demon, removing an evil influencer, or displacing a principality. The process of removing Jezebel's influence over ancient Israel is instructive for our times. There were five major steps in the overall process.

1. Elijah confronted Ahab (1 Kings 17:1).

It all began with a direct confrontation. Ahab had put his trust in the Phoenician god, Baal. Baal had authority to bring rain. Elijah declared there would be no rain. In effect, Baal was rendered powerless. As a result, Ahab lost spiritual control over the nation.

2. The prophets of Baal were confronted before the whole nation (1 Kings 18).

After three years of no rain the prophets of Baal were summoned by Elijah to call down fire on a sacrificial animal. If Baal answered with supernatural fire it would have reasserted his power and control over the nation. The prophets of Baal worked themselves up into a demonic frenzy. Regardless, Baal produced no rain and no fire. Elijah called on the Lord and immediately God answered with fire. A short time after it rained. The defeated prophets of Baal were killed. The removal of the prophets of Baal was hugely significant but it was still only one step in the process of removing Jezebel's influence.

3. King Ahab came under a strong delusion (1 Kings 22:1-40, see also 2 Thessalonians 2:11).

God decided it was time for Ahab to be removed. The prophet Micaiah was shown the heavenly council meeting in which the method of Ahab's removal was decided. One of the participants in the heavenly council offered to become a lying spirit in the mouths of all Ahab's prophets. God agreed. Ahab decided to take back the strategic Israelite city of Ramoth Gilead from the king of Syria. Ahab gathered his prophets. There were about 400 of them. They all prophesied his success in the battle. Only Micaiah prophesied the opposite. Ahab knew that Micaiah was a true prophet of God. Regardless, Ahab was under the influence of a strong delusion and believed the other prophets. Ahab went to battle and died when hit by a random arrow.

4. Ahab's son, King Ahaziah, died through an accident (2 Kings 1).

After Ahab's death, his son Ahaziah ruled in his place for two years. Jezebel continued to exert considerable influence during Ahaziah's reign (1 Kings 22:52-53). Ahaziah injured himself seriously when he fell from his upper room. Ahaziah sent messengers to inquire of Baal whether he would recover or not. The messengers were intercepted by Elijah who declared that Ahaziah would die. Ahaziah sent soldiers to get Elijah. The confrontation between the soldiers and Elijah was dramatic. Twice Elijah called down fire to protect himself. Ahaziah died from his injuries. Elijah was taken up to heaven.

5. A new generation of freedom fighters: Prophets, Kings and Israelites.

Ahaziah had no son so his brother, Jehoram, became king in his place. Jehoram ruled for twelve years. Jezebel had less influence under Jehoram's rule (2 Kings 3:2). During his reign a multi-layered series of events unfolded.

1. Elisha received Elijah's mantle (2 Kings 2).
2. Hazael was anointed as king of Syria (2 Kings 8:7-15).
3. Jehoram was wounded in battle with Hazael (2 Kings 9:14-15).
4. Jehoram withdrew to recover and left Jehu in charge of Israel's army.
5. Jehu was anointed as king of Israel (2 Kings 9:1-13).
6. Jehu killed Jehoram, Jezebel, all the descendants of Ahab, and all the worshipers of Baal (2 Kings 9:14-10:28).

Jezebel's influence was removed from Israel, but it was a dizzying process that played out over a long period of time and on multiple levels. Here were the main players:

- God's heavenly council (1 Kings 22:19-23).
- Elijah, Elisha and Micaiah: Prophets who stood in God's council (1 Kings 17:1, 18:15, 2 Kings 3:14, 5:16).
- Many unnamed prophets: The prophets who Jezebel killed; 100 prophets who remained hidden in two caves (1 Kings 18:4); schools of prophets that were revitalized under Elijah and Elisha's ministries.
- 7000 Israelites who refused to bow their knees to Baal (1 Kings 19:18). Their worship of Yahweh was an act of intercession for the nation.
- An unidentified member of God's heavenly council that became a lying spirit in the mouths of Ahab's prophets.

- A foreign king: Hazael king of Syria.
- A new king: Jehu king of Israel.

God's heavenly council acted and deliberated on behalf of the 7000 Israelites who refused to bow their knees to Baal. Ahab and Jezebel were *ruthless*. The 7000 who didn't bow their knees had *resolve*. It was the resolve of these everyday freedom fighters that determined the destiny of the nation!

THE UNITED STATES AND FREEDOM IN THE NATIONS

In many ways Israel's battle parallels the battle over the destiny and future of the United States of America. The battle is fierce, confusing, messy, and complicated. To understand the times and respond correctly it is necessary to stand in God's council. Even although Elijah stood in God's council, his perspective became skewed when he got caught in the cross-fire of the battle (1 Kings 19:1-18).

This battle is much bigger than casting out a demon, removing an evil influencer, or even displacing a principality. It is about removing "Jezebel's" pervasive influence from the land. Politics, education, music and creative media are major battlefields. New sounds and strategies are being released from heaven. They will carry the authority of decrees released from God's heavenly council. The battle is particularly fierce over the minds and hearts of the emerging generation. A new generation of freedom fighters, both young *and* old, will shift the battle, and determine the outcome.

PRAYER ALERT FOR PRESIDENT TRUMP

(Released 12th October 2019)

At the start of October I was reading Psalm 55. I read down to verse 9, **"For I see violence and strife in the city."** Instantly the Holy Spirit alerted me to the political storm that President Trump is facing. Psalm 55 gives strategic revelation about what is going on and insight about how we can pray. After highlighting Psalm 55 the Holy Spirit reminded me of a prior incidence in my life.

It was the 10th of May 2016. I woke from a dream at 5:59am. The dream was about jealousy between two pastors in the city I was about to visit. Waking at 5:59am was God's way of alerting me to Psalm 55:9, **"For I see violence and strife in the city."** My alarm was set for 6am because I had an early flight to catch. I was flying to another country for a ministry trip but wouldn't arrive at my destination until the next day. After I arrived I was walking to my hotel when I looked up and saw the large digital clock on top of a multi-storied building. Both the time and the temperature were displayed in bright red. The time was 21:21. Underneath was the temperature—21 degrees Celsius. 21 degrees was uncharacteristically cold for the time of year.

"21:21" is a way that God alerts me to divination. Ezekiel 21:21 describes the king of Babylon using divination to consult the will of his gods: **"For the king of Babylon stands at the parting of the road, at the fork of the two roads, to use divination: he shakes the arrows, he consults the images, he looks at the liver" (Ezekiel 21:21).** First I had a dream about jealousy; then I woke from the dream at 5:59am (Psalm 55:9 – violence and strife in the city); then I arrived at my destination and saw the time 21:21 with 21 degrees underneath it (Divination). The combination was hard to ignore. Now you can appreciate why the Holy Spirit reminded me of all this in connection with Psalm 55 and President Trump. Aggressive assignments of jealousy and divination are aligned against the President.

In Psalm 55 David cries out to God with great anguish because of his enemy: **"My thoughts trouble me and I am distraught because of what my enemy is saying, because of the threats of the wicked; for they bring down suffering on me and assail me in their anger" (Psalm 55:2-3).** David was distraught because of what his enemy was saying. The enemies words were demonically empowered. That's where divination comes in. Divination takes human counsel or demonic counsel and speaks it out as if it is God's counsel. Divination empowers false words with such certainty that they seem to come from God Himself. In other words they sound divine. Divination causes false words and false narratives to appear as the truth. The assignment coming against David was so powerful it was even operating through a close friend (Psalm 55:12-14, 20-21).

David graphically describes the situation: **"For I see violence and strife in the city. Day and night they prowl about on its walls; malice and abuse are within it. Destructive forces are at work in the city; threats and lies never leave its streets"**

(Psalm 55:9-11). These words could as easily apply to the present situation in Washington DC. There are two powerful declarations from Psalm 55 that we can speak into the situation:

1. Lord, confuse the wicked and confound their words (Psalm 55:9).
2. Lord, even though many oppose President Trump, rescue him unharmed from the battle waged against him (Psalm 55:18).

Despite the intensity of the situation David was certain God would hear his cry for help: **"Evening, morning and noon I cry out in distress, and he hears my voice" (Psalm 55:17).** Divine help is needed to break the assignments of jealousy and divination that are aligned against the President. What can *we* do? No matter how intense it gets, pray fervently and declare boldly until the truth is revealed and the narrative changes. If the present situation distresses you, let your distress be turned into a continual cry to God. He will hear and respond.

2020:
A YEAR OF SEISMIC SHIFTS

(Released 29th November 2019)

We live in a significant time of transition. Many things are shaking and will continue to shake. Times of transition are often turbulent. Transition is an in-between period. It takes us from one reality or dynamic to another. If we over-focus on the turbulence it's easy to become disorientated. If, instead, we focus on where the transition is taking us, we become prophetic beacons of hope. 2020 is a hugely significant year. It will be marked by several seismic shifts among God's people and within society as a whole.

PROPHETIC MATURITY

Prophets help connect people with the movements, rhythms and sounds of heaven. Seismic shifts happen when the government of heaven comes to earth. Rather than merely having prophetic people within the Church, the Church becomes prophetic.

An army of prophetic people have been maturing and growing. Many in this army are hidden. 2020 marks a milestone in the maturity and promotion of prophetic ministry. Prophetic ministry is "coming of age." In it's infancy prophetic ministry sees things blurry at best. As it matures it sees things with increasing clarity.

"20/20 vision" is a phrase which refers to clarity of vision. Seeing clearly is important. It is even more important to accurately interpret that which is seen. Each prophet sees a part of the whole. There is an increasing humility to look beyond our part and embrace that which others are seeing. Humility means we interpret what we see more accurately.

DIVINE JUSTICE

2020 is a year of divine justice. The two "20"s in 2020 are like the left and right side of a scale used to determine weight. "20" on the left hand side and "20" on the right hand side means the scales are balanced. Where the scales of justice are wrongly weighted one way or the other, God is going to re-calibrate and balance the scales. God's justice is far superior to human justice. His ways are much higher than our ways. His justice often looks vastly different than we expect. The cross is a perfect example of God's unexpected justice. One single act forever changed history. He has ways of doing things that we haven't even perceived yet. In this area we can continue to expect the unexpected.

Justice is a major battlefield and the intensity of the battle will continue to increase. However, when God says, *"Enough is enough,"* everything re-calibrates and the scales of justice become correctly balanced. Not only is God speaking from heaven, He is also raising up a generation that passionately love and seek His ways. They are hardwired for divine justice. From supreme courts over nations to everyday voices on the streets, the voice of divine justice will be heard anew. Major issues of justice will be re-energized with new wisdom, a new tone and new ways of seeing things. Divine justice releases seismic shifts in perceptions, behaviors and even laws.

A GENERATIONAL SHIFT

The Baby Boomer generation has dominated trends throughout its existence. The reason is simple: the Baby Boomer generation—those born from 1946 to 1964—was larger than the generation which preceded it and the generation which followed it. In 2019 the Millennial generation—those born from 1981 to 1996—overtook Baby Boomers as the largest generation. This is a huge generational shift that we can't ignore. 2020 marks the tipping point between the influence of the two generations. The influence of the Baby Boomers will lessen and the influence of Millennials will increase. The differences are already causing friction. This is a seismic shift that has only just started to rumble.

God's heart is inter-generational. That's why Scripture frequently refers to Him as the God of Abraham, the God of Isaac and the God of Jacob. That's three generations tied up in one phrase! God has a plan for each generation. Satan, on the other hand, is always working to bring conflict and misunderstanding between the generations. The Millennial generation is unique, not only because of the world they grew up in, but also because God has made them unique. If the Church fails to understand Millennials it will become increasingly irrelevant.

Recently I woke up in the morning and heard God say, "*I have the wisdom of the ages and wisdom for each age.*" Although the sentence has a double meaning I knew God was emphasizing that

He has wisdom for each stage of life and each new generation that comes forth. The book of Proverbs personifies God's wisdom. If we hear the voice of Wisdom we will capture the attention of Millennials and call them forth to be everything God intended them to be. If we judge them we will fail to discern who they are.

The voice of the Accuser causes rifts between the generations. The voice of Wisdom unifies the generations. Satan intends to use the decreasing influence of Baby Boomers and the increasing influence of Millennials to cause strife and division. We must determine not to be intimidated by the strife. God will give His Church a voice of authority and a voice of love to speak to this generation.

HOW DO WE PREPARE?

It is God who gives understanding of the times and courage to walk in them. We can be intimidated by the turbulence of transition or we can learn to ride the wave of each seismic shift. The best way to prepare is simply to know God's heart:

1. God desires prophetic ministry to grow in love, depth, humility, accuracy and authority.
2. God desires divine justice to re-calibrate and re-balance the scales of justice on the earth.
3. God desires each generation to walk in their prophetic destiny.

As we prepare to step into 2020 let His heartbeat become your heartbeat.

RUSSIA AND GEOPOLITICAL SHIFTS IN THE NATIONS

(Released 8th May 2020)

RUSSIA: A LAND OF PROPHETIC DESTINY

Recently God spoke to me about the nation of Russia. He revealed four things.

Firstly, God has a redemptive and prophetic call over Russia. She has a strategic role in His plan for the nations.

Secondly, the relationship between Russia and the United States is an important one.

Thirdly, I heard two questions in the spirit realm:

1. *"Can Russia be trusted?"*
2. *"Do you see Russia as I see her?"*

The first question was coming from individuals and nations. The second question was coming from God.

Fourthly, God's intention is to bring down the dividing wall between Russia and the West.

Sometimes the way God reveals things to us is as significant as the revelations themselves. God revealed these four things to me over several days. The sequence is significant. The process starts by seeing God's redemptive and prophetic call over Russia as a nation.

There are many things that shape our perceptions about nations, such as history, current events, and theological systems of thought. Our existing perceptions can make it hard for us to see nations through God's eyes. Add to this the fact that Satan works overtime to sow seeds of distrust between nations—particularly those with strategic relationships. There is a level of unity, understanding and co-operation between Russia and the United States that Satan fears.

Many are asking, *"Can Russia be trusted?"* In the midst of the questioning God says, *"Russia is in My hands. Can I not turn the heart of a king, or the heart of a nation for My purposes? Can I not change the heart of a nation in a day? Nations naturally act for their own interests, but watch, for Russia shall also act for Mine"* (see Proverbs 21:1, Isaiah 66:8).

RUSSIA'S CHRISTIAN FOUNDATIONS

Russia has strong Christian foundations. Christianity came to Kievan Rus (a loose federation of peoples in north eastern Europe) in 988 when Vladimir the Great was baptized. This is widely seen as the birth of the Russian Orthodox Church. In 1054 a major separation—known as the East-West Schism—

took place between Eastern and Western Christianity. This religious schism forms part of the back story to the modern geopolitical divide between Russia and the West. Today the Eastern Orthodox Church comprises about 300 million people. The Russian Orthodox Church—with about 150 million—is by far the largest of the Eastern Orthodox churches.

The Russian novelists and writers Fyodor Dostoevsky (1821-1881), Leo Tolstoy (1828-1910) and Aleksandr Solzhenitsyn (1918-2008) are considered giants of literature. Their writings are also reputed for their prophetic stature. These men were radical for their times. Eventually their words shifted cultures and changed nations. To cite one example: Tolstoy had a great influence on Mahatma Gandhi. Gandhi in turn had a great influence on Martin Luther King Jr.

GEOPOLITICAL SHIFTS IN THE NATIONS

The message of God's kingdom is revolutionary. Men and women, and even boys and girls, of prophetic stature will arise in Russia. They will release a prophetic fire that will ignite Russia and spill over into other nations. The combination of prophetic voices from Russia and the West will bring a sharper prophetic discernment than before. The dividing wall between Russia and the West will come down. This will cause major geopolitical shifts in the earth.

Many of the geopolitical shifts that are coming are not even on people's radars, few perceive them. God is revealing these to His people so that we can intercede and call forth His higher purposes. He wants us to become familiar with the fault-lines within nations and between nations so that we can decree His purposes. Many things look one way on the earth, but very different when viewed from God's vantage point. It's time to see what He sees and decree what He tells us. As we do this, nations will be realigned and called into unprecedented and unrealized destiny.

PENTECOST 2020: A SIGNIFICANT DEMARCATION POINT FOR THE CHURCH

(Released 27th May 2020)

2020 is a year of major transition. During Easter 2020 the world was largely shut down due to fear. During the first Easter the disciples lived in great fear—they fled when the authorities arrested Jesus and remained hidden after Jesus' resurrection (Mark 14:50, John 20:19, 26). 50 days after Easter was the feast of Pentecost. Holy Spirit invaded 120 praying believers in an upper room. The fledgling church was empowered with great boldness despite strong opposition. Likewise, in 2020, we are moving from the fear and uncertainty of Easter, to the faith and certainty of Pentecost. Pentecost 2020 is a significant demarcation point for the church.

THE CONNECTION WITH ANOINTED PROPHETS

One of the main manifestations of the Pentecost outpouring was prophecy, visions and dreams (Acts 2:17-18). It's important to understand the Jewish mindset. Prophecy, visions and dreams were the domain of prophets. Through their decrees prophets released words that shaped cities and nations. Now, instead of this anointing being poured out on a select few, it would be poured out on all who would receive it. Even menservants and maidservants would be entrusted with this unique authority. The church was empowered with:

1. Authority to decree God's purposes.
2. Authority to live the dreams and visions they received.
3. Authority to shape cities and nations.
4. Authority to shake the heavens and the earth (Acts 2:19-20).
5. Authority to reap the "harvest fields" of the nations for Jesus (Acts 2:21).

The impact was immediate. Jerusalem was filled with their teaching, disciples were multiplied greatly, many priests were obedient to the faith (Acts 5:28, 6:7).

THE CONNECTION WITH THE MINISTRY OF JESUS

The gospel of Luke and the book of Acts were both written by Luke. A deliberate connection is made between Jesus' empowerment for supernatural ministry and believers empowerment to do the same. Luke records Jesus' baptism by John the Baptist: **"And the Holy Spirit descended in bodily form like a dove upon Him, and a voice came from heaven which said, 'You are My beloved Son; in You I am well** pleased'" **(Luke 3:22).** Note particularly the involvement of the Father, Jesus and the Holy Spirit in this scene.

Speaking about the outpouring on the day of Pentecost Peter declared: **"This Jesus God has raised up, of which we are all witnesses. Therefore being exalted to the right hand of God, and having received from the Father the promise of the Holy Spirit, He poured out this which you now see and hear"** **(Acts 2:32-33).** The mention of the Father, Jesus and the Holy Spirit makes a deliberate connection back to Jesus' baptism and empowerment for earthly ministry. At Pentecost believers were anointed to continue the supernatural ministry of Jesus. As one commentator says, "He who had earlier received the Spirit for the public discharge of His own earthly ministry had now received that same Spirit to impart to His representatives, in order that they might continue, and indeed share in, the ministry which He had begun" (F. F. Bruce, *New International Commentary of the New Testament*).

THE CONNECTION WITH GOD'S THRONE

The Pentecost outpouring had a connection with anointed prophets and the anointed ministry of Jesus, but it gets even better. Acts 2:33, quoted above, connects the outpouring of Pentecost with a threefold blessing:

1. **The faithfulness and generosity of the Father.** Jesus received from the Father the promise of the Holy Spirit for us.

2. **The authority and generosity of Jesus.**
    Jesus was exalted to the highest seat of authority next to the Father. From this position He poured out the Holy Spirit.

3. **The extravagance and generosity of the Holy Spirit poured out in a tangible way.**
    The outpouring was tangible—it could be seen and heard. The outpouring was extravagant—many mocked and said, **"They are drunk with new wine!" (Acts 2:13).**

This threefold blessing is our inheritance. It connects us with the highest level of authority and the highest level of generosity. This authority and generosity flows through all who receive the fullness of the Spirit. Unfortunately many have equated the Pentecost outpouring with an experience. It was much much more than just an experience. It was directly connected with a throne.

THE WONDERFUL WORKS OF GOD

Thousands were gathered at Jerusalem for the feast of Pentecost. They had come from all the surrounding nations. 120 praying believers received the outpouring and immediately began to declare the wonderful works of God (Acts 2:11). Thousands were impacted with the same authority and the same generosity. They took it with them as they returned to their respective nations. The Church turned the tide in the nations.

A lot of negative news has been released over the last few months. Fear has gone out into the highways and byways.

People live in fear of sickness, financial hardship and economic collapse. Pentecost 2020 marks a significant time of demarcation. Pentecost gave the early church a voice. The destiny of nations was forever changed. Fear was turned into faith. The lame walked (Acts 3:1-10). Shadows healed the sick (Acts 5:12-16). Financial miracles became common place (Acts 4:33-37). The authority of this outpouring isn't just for our personal blessing—it will shape cities and nations. It's time to declare the wonderful works of God.

THE LION IS ROARING

(Released 5th June 2020)

2020 is a year of divine justice. In the days of Amos the prophet, God roared against injustice:

"The LORD roars from Zion and thunders from Jerusalem" (Amos 1:2).

"The lion has roared—who will not fear? The Sovereign LORD has spoken— who can but prophesy?" (Amos 3:8).

"Let justice roll on like a river, righteousness like a never-failing stream!" (Amos 5:24).

Although Amos was from the southern kingdom of Judah he preached in the northern kingdom of Israel. After the reign of King Solomon, the northern kingdom split from the southern kingdom over the issue of oppression and forced labor (1 Kings 12:1-20). Now, less than 200 years later, Israel was guilty of oppressing her own poor (Amos 2:7-8, 4:1, 5:11-12, 8:4-6). Greed and dishonest gain had replaced justice and righteousness. God roared. Israel was scattered.

The United States of America has this in common with the northern kingdom of Israel: both nations were formed because people desired to live free from oppression. God's plan is not to "scatter" the United States, but rather to heal the wounds of injustice that afflict the nation. As these wounds are healed, the United States will gain greater strength and standing in the nations.

Almost 2000 years ago, during the feast of Pentecost, God visited 120 believers in Jerusalem. Empowered by the Spirit, they boldly spoke with new tongues and declared the wonderful works of God (Acts 2:4, 11). Jews had gathered from many nations. They heard the declarations in their own languages. 3000 were saved in one day (Acts 2:41). Many newly saved disciples returned to their respective nations, extending God's offer of salvation and reconciliation through their witness.

Pentecost was the antithesis of Babel. At the tower of Babel a united humanity, with a common language, rebelled against God (Genesis 11:1-9). God came down, confused their language, and scattered the people. At Pentecost God came down, overcame language barriers, and initiated a great in-gathering. God roared at Pentecost. This roar was to gather, not scatter. The roar continued to reverberate through His people and among the nations. Pentecost gave the newly formed Church a voice. Dividing walls came down.

Pentecost 2020 marks a significant point of demarcation for the church and for the nations. Once again God is roaring against injustice. In the United States, Pentecost 2020 was marked by riots after the outrageous death of black man, George Floyd, at the hands of a white police officer. In the United States God's roar is about to be felt by the black community. He is roaring over them and will roar through them. It will be seen, heard and felt. This roar will bring healing and impart identity and courage.

A new sound of heavenly justice will come forth. It will look different than anything the nation has seen before. There will be tears and rejoicing in the streets. What the enemy meant for evil will be turned for good. God's message to the black community is this: *"I have not forgotten you. I heard the cries of your grandfathers and grandmothers. Their intercession was precious to Me. Don't be ashamed at the depth of your pain. As you pour it out I will heal the reproach of many generations. I have called you for such a time as this."*

In his generation Martin Luther King released a prophetic message from heaven. Since that time many agendas have tried to usurp and clutter this message. God's roar will restore the purity, the power, and the simplicity of the message. As healing comes, the United States will be renewed with fresh vision and fresh clarity. She will be stirred once again to fulfill her God-ordained mandate of bringing freedom to the nations. Martin Luther King didn't just *speak* a message, his life *was* a message. In this generation that message will be multiplied and trumpeted through the lives of many many people.

Heavenly justice and earthly justice often look totally different. In the midst of the present chaos and protests, God has a plan. **"Surely the Sovereign LORD does nothing without revealing His plan to his servants the prophets. The lion has roared— who will not fear? The Sovereign LORD has spoken— who can but prophesy?" (Amos 3:7-8).** Only as we get close to His heart can we release and call forth the sound of divine justice for this generation.

BELIEVING IN MIRACLES IS A GIFT FROM GOD

(Released 11th September 2020)

Four years ago I heard Donald Trump make the statement, *"It's gonna be HUGE!"* A few weeks later I was praying for this generation and I heard God say, *"It's gonna be HUGE!"* Suddenly the phrase was loaded with prophetic significance. God has big plans for this generation. On the 25th of August 2020 Tiffany Trump said, *"Believing in miracles is a gift from God."* When I heard the phrase I instantly knew its prophetic significance. Believing in miracles is a gift God is releasing to a new generation. Interestingly, the name Tiffany comes from the Greek "theophania" which means "a manifestation or appearance of God." Throughout history the enemies of God's people change, but the mandate to reveal God in supernatural ways does not.

In Gideon's day the Israelites lived in continual fear of their Midianite oppressors. In order to protect his harvest from being taken, Gideon threshed his wheat in a winepress! A winepress was a cavity cut out of rock. It was the most unlikely place to thresh wheat. Normally wheat was threshed at a threshing floor located outside the city, and with a threshing sledge pulled by animals. Gideon threshed with a stick, in a winepress, inside the city. It goes without saying: Gideon's circumstances were limiting.

Despite the unusual situation, events took an even more unusual turn. As Gideon continued to beat the wheat the angel of the Lord appeared to him announcing, **"The LORD is with you, mighty warrior" (Judges 6:12).** Incredulous, Gideon replied, **"If the LORD is with us, why then has all this happened to us? And where are all His miracles which our fathers told us about" (Judges 6:13).** The oppression of the Midianites had caused Israel to cry out to God (Judges 6:6). God not only heard their cry, but set Himself to take action. It was time for miracles. All God had to work with was an unbelieving man and an unbelieving nation. Gideon didn't understand three things: (1) the time; (2) the gift of miracles; and (3) his identity as a mighty warrior. God chose Gideon to rout an army of 135,000 with an army of only 300—a ratio of 1 to 450 (Judges 7:7, 8:10)! Miracles were the means that God used to bring about national deliverance.

Over a thousand years later a vastly different situation arose. God used Peter and John to heal a lame man. The man had been lame since birth and was over 40 years old when the miracle took place (Acts 3:1-10, 4:22). Because it was such an astonishing and very public miracle, word spread to all of Jerusalem. Unlike Gideon, Peter and John were not contending with a foreign army. Their opposition came from a combination of religious and political forces (Acts 4:1, 5-6). Peter and John were arrested. The religious and political leaders had a major problem on their hands because the man who had been healed was standing among them for all to see. **"What shall we do to these men? For, indeed, that a notable miracle has been done through them is evident to all who dwell in**

Jerusalem, and we cannot deny it" (Acts 4:16). Peter and John were eventually released, but under threat not to speak in Jesus' name.

Peter and John and their companions went straight to prayer. They understood the cosmic battle taking place: **"Lord, You are God, who made heaven and earth and the sea, and all that is in them, who by the mouth of Your servant David have said: 'Why did the nations rage, and the people plot vain things? The kings of the earth took their stand, and the rulers were gathered together against the Lord and against His Christ'" (Acts 4:24-26).** They prayed boldly, **"Now, Lord, look on their threats, and grant to Your servants that with all boldness they may speak Your word, by stretching out Your hand to heal, and that signs and wonders may be done through the name of Your holy Servant Jesus" (Acts 4:29-30).** Why did they pray this way? Because they understood the times, the gift of miracles, and their identity as mighty warriors.

Miracles are God's specialty. Through them He brings deliverance to individuals and nations—destinies and outcomes are radically changed. God is looking for people of faith and vision. Galatians 3:5 makes it clear: God supplies the Spirit to us; He works miracles among us; and He does this, not by the works of the law, but by the hearing of faith. Believing in miracles is a gift from God being released to this generation. They will understand the times, the gift of miracles, and, their identity as mighty warriors. Threats may rage. Miracles will speak. History will be changed.

It's gonna be HUGE!

IT'S TIME FOR THE CHURCH TO HAVE A VOICE

(Released 25th September 2020)

Pentecost gave the Church a voice. The voice had authority. The voice penetrated to the heart of Jerusalem (Acts 5:28, 6:7). People had two options: hear the voice or resist the voice. There was no force or manipulative coercion. Each person had to make their own free will decision. Those who responded to the voice were radically transformed. The motives of those who resisted the voice were exposed. Because Jerusalem was a governmental center the impact began to shake and shift the nation. Persecution only multiplied the impact.

There are many voices in modern Christendom. It's important that we understand where each voice comes from. James makes it abundantly clear: **"Human anger does not produce the righteousness that God desires" (James 1:20 NIV).** Many voices come from anger, frustration, impatience and striving. The original Pentecost was different. Their voice resonated not with human anger, but with heavenly mandate. We must discern the difference. The problem is this: Anger makes us feel righteous. Righteous anger is much rarer than people realize. In fact the foundational revelation about God's anger is that He is slow to anger (Exodus 34:6, Numbers 14:18, Nehemiah 9:17,

Psalm 86:15, 103:8, 145:8, Joel 2:13, Jonah 4:2, Nahum 1:3). Let's be honest, our zeal can be rooted in anger, or love, but most often both.

James describes the characteristics of the voice that resonated from Pentecost: **"The wisdom that comes from heaven is first of all pure; then peace-loving, considerate, submissive, full of mercy and good fruit, impartial and sincere" (James 3:17 NIV).** That doesn't mean it wasn't confrontational, direct, clear and in-your-face. It was all of those thing, but most importantly, it resonated with something that was heavenly, not earthly. Paul says in Colossians 3:1-2, **"Since, then, you have been raised with Christ, set your hearts on things above, where Christ is, seated at the right hand of God. Set your minds on things above, not on earthly things."** Christ is seated at the right hand of God. This language describes a governmental seat. That's why when we connect with Christ our voices have authority.

There are two things we need to beware of: the political spirit and the religious spirit. In fact these two forces usually work hand-in-glove. Is God interested in politics? The simple answer is yes. He is interested in politics because He is interested in people. Politics and policies impact people. As Christians we shouldn't be frightened to have a voice in the political arena, however, we must guard against yielding to a political spirit. Religious and political spirits feign righteousness. They then force others to take sides. Religious and political forces can deceive even the discerning. When a clear sound comes from heaven it cuts through the fog of confusion and helps people see and know the truth. They can then make free will decisions. A political or religious spirit will try and bind people to its perspective and insist that people join a particular party or way of thinking.

Are we too frightened to have a voice and be a voice? Are we intimidated by the chaos and confusion created by politics and the media? Jesus has a clear perspective and clear voice. We are connected to Him and His voice resonates through us. If we listen for His voice it will penetrate through the cacophony of chaotic sounds clamoring for our attention. The voice that comes from heaven cuts through earthly agendas and re-orientates people toward heavenly ones. It's time for the Church to have a voice!

EPILOGUE: A NEW BREED OF REVOLUTIONARIES

2000 years ago a revolution started with a single man. John the Baptist didn't come with a theology, he came with a cry. The cry had three parts to it:

1. Behold the King!
2. Behold the Lamb!
3. Behold the Bridegroom!

The cry grabbed the attention of a generation.

The message of the King and His kingdom was foundational to John's cry: **"Repent for the kingdom of heaven is here!" (Matthew 3:2).** But Jesus was more than a king. The moment John set eyes on Jesus a deeper cry erupted from within him: **"Behold! The Lamb of God who takes away the sin of the world!" (John 1:29).** The king was also a lamb. But that was not all.

John's eyes penetrated deeper yet. He understood that Jesus was a bridegroom: **"He who has the bride is the bridegroom; but**

the friend of the bridegroom, who stands and hears him, rejoices greatly because of the bridegroom's voice. Therefore this joy of mine is fulfilled" (John 3:29). "King," "lamb," "bridegroom" and "bride" are part of the rich landscape of biblical imagery. A king rules. A lamb lays down its life. A bridegroom is passionately in love.

John the Baptist was merely a forerunner. There is a new breed of revolutionaries arising. There is a new cry in the land. The cry reverberates with the unrelenting rhythm of a passionate heart beat:

"Behold the King!"

"Behold the Lamb!"

"Behold the Bridegroom!"

This army of freedom fighters is made up of men and women, boys and girls. They don't come with a theology—they come with a cry. They have been awakened by the spirit of wisdom and revelation in the knowledge of Jesus. They have seen *Him*—and when you see Him as He is, you can never get away from Him. They have become mesmerized with Jesus.

United States, it's time for a new breed of freedom fighters to arise. There's only two questions to consider: Can you hear the cry? And will you enlist?

ABOUT THE AUTHOR

Nathan Shaw helps bring individuals and churches into dynamic encounters with God's indescribable love. His passion is to equip churches so that they can move in the Spirit, access heavenly realms, encounter God's heart and release His kingdom on the earth. Over the last 26 years he has been instrumental in ushering in significant moves of the Spirit in 12 different nations. Many have experienced life changing prophetic encounters and dramatic visitations from God.

Nathan is the author of *Passion and Fire* and *Unto the Least of These*. *Passion and Fire* tells the story of a powerful move of the Spirit in the South Pacific nation of Vanuatu, during which the face of Jesus appeared on a dormitory wall. *Unto the Least of These* is about God's incredible love for widows and the fatherless and the significant part they play in His end-time plans. Both books are acclaimed by respected leaders from across the body of Christ.

Nathan is the founder of Heart of David Ministries and the founder and pastor of Celebration Church in Mosgiel, New Zealand.

PROPHETIC AND TEACHING BULLETIN

Receive timely prophetic and teaching articles

Sign up at www.heartofdavidministries.org

SUBSCRIBE TO
HEART OF DAVID MINISTRIES
YOUTUBE CHANNEL

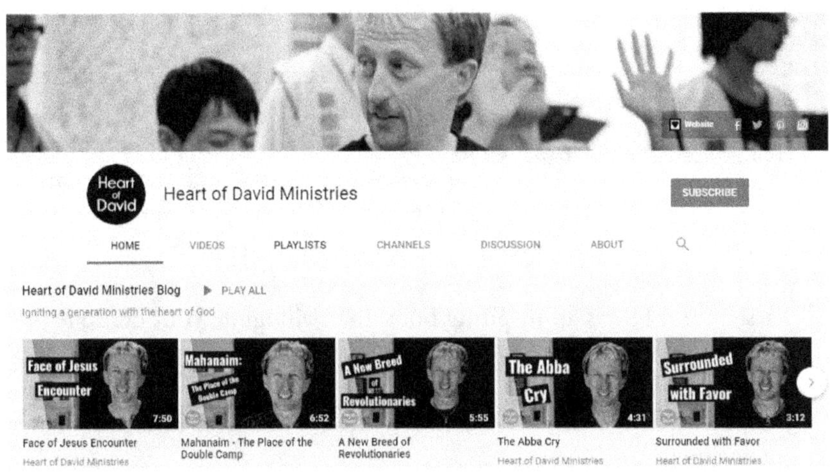

www.youtube.com/heartofdavidvid

Passion And Fire –
Igniting Your Passion For God

God is a consuming fire. He calls out to us, inviting us into a passionate relationship with Him.

Across the Church, there is a growing sense of dissatisfaction with religion, and an increasing desire for greater intimacy with God and purpose in living. Living with such intimacy and purpose is not an unobtainable dream.

In Passion and Fire, Nathan Shaw communicates God's love for us and describes what an on-going encounter with God can be like. He explains how our relationship with God can fuel our love for others and enable us to reach out beyond our boundaries.

Passion and Fire is an inspiring book that will ignite your desire for God.

"A spiritual accelerant that will ignite a fresh burden for intimacy and involvement."

> – David Ravenhill, Author and Bible teacher

Available as ebook or paperback

Order from Amazon, Book Depository or Heart of David Ministries

Amazon Author Page
www.amazon.com/Nathan-Shaw/e/B001KHL646/

Unto The Least Of These –
Expressing God's Love To Widows And The Fatherless

Widows, divorcees and the fatherless are some of the loneliest people on earth. Nathan Shaw has a heart for this disenfranchised portion of Christ's Church and presents healing words to those who are brokenhearted. He issues a challenge for all Christians to mirror the Father's heart to those who are hurting and vulnerable.

"Nathan makes us painfully aware how we have not only not succored widows and orphans, but we have actually increased their sufferings by our judgments, both expressed and undercurrent."
– John Loren Sandford, Elijah House

"A clarion call for us to draw near to God and let His concern become our concern... a cutting edge message for the twenty-first century."
– Mike Bickle, International House of Prayer

Available as ebook or paperback

Order from Amazon or Heart of David Ministries

Amazon Author Page
www.amazon.com/Nathan-Shaw/e/B001KHL646/

BETRAYED! (BOOKLET)

Betrayal is one of the deepest and most excruciating wounds a person can experience.

Above everything else, human beings are created with a capacity and yearning to know relational depth and intimacy. That is why abandonment and betrayal rip and scar the human heart so deeply. Whether you have been abandoned or betrayed by a friend, a marriage partner or a parent, *Betrayed!* will minister healing and hope on your journey of recovery.

"My heart was warmed by the compassion and love that I (coming from a broken home and raised by a single mother) felt when I read *Betrayed!* This booklet will bring healing to those with holes in their souls."

– John A. Kilpatrick

Available as ebook

Order from Amazon

Amazon Author Page
www.amazon.com/Nathan-Shaw/e/B001KHL646/

Invite Nathan To Speak at Your Church or Conference

Contact details at www.heartofdavidministries.org

PASSION AND FIRE MEETINGS

God is supernatural. He wants to radically encounter every one of us, not just the few who seem more spiritual. His supernatural river of fiery love awakens holy passion in our hearts and makes us unstoppable.

Live on fire | Live in the supernatural | It's your destiny!

EAGLE TRAINING SCHOOLS

A hands on supernatural school that will equip, anoint, sharpen and prepare you for the end-time harvest.

Eagle Training Schools can be as simple as a few meetings or something more substantial lasting several days.

HEART OF DAVID MINISTRIES

HEART OF DAVID MINISTRIES HAS A SINGULAR PASSION--TO IGNITE A GENERATION WITH THE HEART OF GOD.

IT IS OUR PRAYER THAT GOD'S RIVER OF FIERY LOVE WILL OVERWHELM YOU--AND THEN OVERFLOW THROUGH YOU.

Visit us online for...

- Prophetic and Teaching Articles
- Audio
- Video
- Books
- Social Media Links

www.heartofdavidministries.org